You Can Crochet Socks™

General Information

Many of the products used in this pattern book can be purchased from local craft, fabric and variety stores, or from the Annie's Attic Needlecraft Catalog (see Customer Service information on page 15).

Contents

Chocolate-Covered Cherries

SKILL LEVEL

FINISHED SIZES

Instructions given fit size small *(women's shoe size 6–7)*; changes for size medium *(women's shoe size 8–10)* and size large *(women's shoe size 12–14)* are in [ ].

MATERIALS

- Red Heart LusterSheen fine (sport) weight yarn (4 oz/335 yds/113g per skein):
  1 skein each #0913 warm red and #0360 chocolate

- Size C/2/2.75mm crochet hook or size needed to obtain gauge
- Tapestry needle
- Stitch markers

GAUGE

20 sc = 4 inches; 27 sc rows = 4 inches

PATTERN NOTE

Weave in ends as work progresses.

INSTRUCTIONS

SOCK

MAKE 2.

TOE

***Note:** Toe is worked in continuous rnds. After placing markers, move them as you come to them.*

With warm red, ch 9 [9, 13], sc in 2nd ch from hook, sc in each of next 6 [6, 10] chs, 3 sc in next ch, place marker in 2nd sc, working in unused lps on opposite side of beg ch, sc in each of next 6 [6, 10] lps, 2 sc in last lp, place marker in last sc made, *2 sc in next sc, sc in each sc across to first sc before next marker, 2 sc in next sc, sc in marked sc, rep from * until there are 44 [50, 56] sc, sc in each sc to next marker, **change color** *(see Stitch Guide)* to chocolate in last sc, cut warm red. Remove markers.

FOOT

***Note:** Foot is worked in continuous rnds. After placing markers, move them as you come to them.*

Sc in each sc around until piece measures 6 [6½, 7] inches from beg or 2 inches shorter than length of foot from heel to toe.

HEEL FLAP

Fold piece having Toe flat. Place markers in sc at folds having 21 [24, 27] sc between markers.

Row 1 (RS): Sc in each sc to next marker, change color to warm red in last sc, **do not cut chocolate,** turn.

Row 2: Ch 1, sc in each of first 21 [24, 27] sc, ch 1, turn.

Rows 3–13: Rep row 2.

TURN HEEL

Row 1: Ch 1, sc in each of first 14 [16, 18] sc, **sc dec** *(see Stitch Guide)* in next 2 sc, turn. *(15 [17, 19] sc)*

Row 2: Ch 1, sc in each of first 8 [9, 10] sc, sc dec in next sc and in next sc on row 13 of Heel Flap, turn. *(9 [10, 11] sc)*

Rep row 2 until all sc on row 13 are worked.

GUSSET

Row 1: Ch 1, sk first sc, sc in each of next 7 [8, 9] sc, work 10 [12, 14] sc evenly spaced across ends of rows of Heel Flap, change color to chocolate in last sc, carry warm red, place marker in last sc, sc in each of next 23 [26, 29] sc, place marker in last sc, work 10 [12, 14] sc evenly spaced across ends of rows of Heel Flap. *(50 [58, 66] sc)*

Now working in continuous rnds, *sc in each sc to 2 sc before next marker, sc dec in next 2 sc, sc in each sc to next marker, sc in marked sc, sc dec in next 2 sc, rep from * until there are 44 [53, 62] sc, sc in each sc to next marker.

ANKLE

Note: *Ankle is worked in continuous rnds. Keep last marker to mark end of following rnds. Remove other marker.*

Rnd 1: Sc in each of next 3 sc, 3 sc in next sc, sc in each of next 3 sc, *sk next 2 sc, sc in each of next 3 sc, 3 sc in next sc, sc in each of next 3 sc, rep from * to last sc, sk last sc. *(44 [53, 62] sc)*

Rnd 2: Sk first sc, sc in each of next 3 sc, 3 sc in next sc, sc in each of next 3 sc, *sk next 2 sc, sc in each of next 3 sc, 3 sc in next sc, sc in each of next 3 sc, rep from * to last sc, sk last sc. *(44 [53, 62] sc)*

Rep rnd 2 in following color stripe pattern: 1 rnd chocolate, 1 rnd warm red, 1 rnd chocolate, 2 rnds warm red, 3 rnds chocolate, 5 rnds warm red, 3 rnds chocolate, 2 rnds warm red, 1 rnd chocolate, 1 rnd warm red.

At end of last rnd, join with sl st in first sc. Fasten off both colors. ■

Berries

SKILL LEVEL

INTERMEDIATE

FINISHED SIZES

Instructions given fit size small *(women's shoe size 6–7)*; changes for size medium *(women's shoe size 8–10)* and size large *(women's shoe size 12–14)* are in [ ].

MATERIALS

- Patons Kroy Socks super fine (sock) weight yarn (1¾ oz/203 yds/50g per balls:
  2 [2, 3] balls #54561 winter eclipse
- Size C/2/2.75mm crochet hook or size needed to obtain gauge
- Tapestry needle
- Stitch markers

1 SUPER FINE

GAUGE

25 sc = 4 inches; 27 sc rows = 4 inches
Take time to check gauge.

PATTERN NOTE

Weave in ends as work progresses.

INSTRUCTIONS

SOCK

MAKE 2.

TOE

Note: *Toe is worked in continuous rnds. After placing markers, move them as you come to them.*

Ch 11 [13, 15], sc in 2nd ch from hook, sc in each of next 8 [10, 12] chs, 3 sc in next ch, place marker in 2nd sc of 3 sc just made, working in unused lps on opposite side of beg ch, sc in each of next 8 [10, 12] lps, 2 sc in last lp, place marker, *2 sc in next sc, sc in each sc across to 1 sc before next marker, 2 sc in next sc, sc in marked sc, rep from * until there are 44 [50, 56] sc.

FOOT

Note: *Foot is worked in continuous rnds. After placing markers, move them as you come to them.*

Sc in each sc around until piece measures 6 [6½, 7] inches from beg or 2 inches shorter than length of foot from heel to toe.

HEEL OPENING

Fold piece having Toe flat, sc in each sc to fold, ch 26 [29, 32], sk next 22 [25, 28] sc, sc in next sc. *(48 [54, 60] sc)*

ANKLE

Sc in each sc around until piece measures 4 [4½, 6] inches from beg of Ankle. Fasten off.

HEEL

Join yarn with sl st at side of Heel Opening, work 50 [56, 62] sc evenly spaced around Opening. **Do not join.** Place marker at each side of Opening having 24 [27, 30] sc between markers.

*Sc in each sc to 2 sc before next marker, **sc dec** *(see Stitch Guide)* in next 2 sts, sc in marked sc, sc dec in next 2 sc, rep from * until 20 [24, 28] sc remain. Fasten off.

FINISHING

Turn Sock inside out. Sew Heel Opening closed.■

Key Lime

SKILL LEVEL

INTERMEDIATE

FINISHED SIZES

Instructions given fit size small *(women's shoe size 6–7)*; changes for size medium *(women's shoe size 8–10)* and size large *(women's shoe size 12–14)* are in [ ].

MATERIALS

- Lion Brand Microspun light (DK) weight yarn (2½ oz/168 yds/70g per ball):
  2 [2, 3] balls #194 lime
- Size F/5/3.75mm crochet hook or size needed to obtain gauge
- Tapestry needle
- Stitch markers

3 LIGHT

GAUGE

18 sc = 4 inches; 18 sc rows = 4 inches
Take time to check gauge

PATTERN NOTE

Weave in ends as work progresses.

SPECIAL STITCHES

Beg single crochet foundation stitch (beg sc foundation st): Ch 2, insert hook in 2nd ch from hook, yo, draw lp through, yo, draw through 1 lp on hook *(base ch)*, yo, draw through 2 lps on hook.

Single crochet foundation stitch (sc foundation st): Insert hook in base ch of indicated st, yo, draw lp through, yo, draw through 1 lp on hook *(base ch)*, yo, draw through 2 lps on hook.

Cluster (cl): Insert hook in next st, yo, draw lp through, insert in first ch of next ch-2 sp, yo, draw lp through, insert hook under 2nd ch of same ch-2 sp, yo, draw lp through, yo, draw through all 4 lps on hook.

INSTRUCTIONS

SOCK

MAKE 2.

CUFF

Beg sc foundation st *(see Special Stitches)*, 42 [47, 53] **sc foundation sts** *(see Special Stitches)*, to join, being careful not to twist sts, draw up lp in each of first 3 sts, yo and draw through all 4 lps on hook.

Note: *Remainder of Cuff is worked in continuous rnds. Do not join.*

Rnd 1: Ch 2, ***sc dec** *(see Stitch Guide)* in next 3 sts, ch 2, rep from * around.

Rnd 2: ***Cl** *(see Special Stitches)* in next st and in 2 chs of next ch-2 sp, ch 2, rep from * around.

Rep rnd 2 until piece measures 6 inches from beg.

HEEL

Row 1: Now working in rows, [Cl, ch 2] 10 [11, 12] times, sc in each of next 21 [24, 27] sts, turn.

Row 2: Ch 1, sc in each sc across, turn.

Rep row 2 until piece measures 2 inches from beg of Heel, ending with a WS row.

TURN HEEL

Row 1 (RS): Ch 1, sc in each of first 14 [16, 18] sc, sc dec in next 2 sc, turn. *(15 [17, 19] sc)*

Row 2: Ch 1, sk first sc, sc in each of next 7 [8, 9] sc, sc dec in next sc and in next sc on last row of Heel, turn. *(8 [9, 10] sc)*

Rep row 2 until all sc on last row of Heel are worked.

GUSSET

Rnd 1 (RS): Ch 1, sk first sc, sc in each of next 7 [8, 9] sc, work 10 [12, 14] sc evenly spaced across end of rows of Heel, place marker, [cl, ch 2] 7 [8, 9] times, place marker, work 10 [12, 14] sc evenly spaced across end of rows of Heel. *(49 [56, 63] sc)*

Rnd 2: *Sc in each sc to 2 sc before next marker, sc dec in next 2 sc, sc in next sc, place marker, work top of Gusset in pattern, place marker, sc in next sc, sc dec in next 2 sc, rep from * 5 times. *(39 [46, 53] sc)*

FOOT

Continue working pattern on top of foot section and sc in each sc on sole section until piece measures 11 [12, 14] inches from beg of Cuff or 2 inches shorter than length of wearer's foot.

TOE

Place marker in first and last sc of Foot having 18 [22, 25] sc between markers, sc across Foot, sc dec in 2 sts before and after each marker until 14 [16, 18] sc remain. Fasten off.

FINISHING

Turn Sock inside out. Sew end of Toe closed. ■

Tropical Punch

SKILL LEVEL

FINISHED SIZES

Instructions given fit size small *(women's shoe size 6–7)*; changes for size medium *(women's shoe size 8–10)* and size large *(women's shoe size 12–14)* are in [ ].

MATERIALS

- Light (light worsted) weight yarn: 7 [7, 10½] oz/140 [140, 210] yds/198 [198, 297] g turquoise multi
- Size F/5/3.75mm crochet hook or size needed to obtain gauge
- Tapestry needle
- Stitch markers

GAUGE

19 sc = 4 inches; 21 sc rows = 4 inches
Take time to check gauge.

PATTERN NOTES

Weave in ends as work progresses.
Chain-3 at beg of double crochet rounds counts as a back post double crochet.

SPECIAL STITCHES

Beg double crochet foundation stitch (beg dc foundation st): Ch 3, yo, insert hook in 3rd ch from hook, yo, draw lp through, yo, draw through 1 lp on hook *(base ch)*, [yo, draw through 2 lps on hook] twice.

Double crochet foundation stitch (dc foundation st): *Yo, insert hook in base ch of indicated st, yo, draw lp through, yo, draw through 1 lp on hook *(base ch)*, [yo, draw through 2 lps on hook] twice.

INSTRUCTIONS

SOCK
MAKE 2.
CUFF

Foundation rnd: **Beg dc foundation st** *(see Special Stitches)*, 34 [38, 42] **dc foundation sts** *(see Special Stitches)*, being careful not to twist sts, join with sl st in 3rd ch of beg ch-3.

Rnd 1: **Ch 3** *(see Pattern Notes)*, **fpdc** *(see Stitch Guide)* around next st, ***bpdc** *(see Stitch Guide)* around next st, fpdc around next st, rep from * around, join in 3rd ch of beg ch-3. *(36 [40, 44] sts)*

Rep rnd 1 until piece measures 4 inches from beg.

HEEL

Row 1: Now working in rows, ch 1, sc in each of first 9 [10, 11] sts, place marker, sc in each of next 18 [20, 22] sts, place marker, turn. *(27 [30, 33] sc)*

Row 2: Sc in each of first 17 [19, 21] sc, leaving rem sts unworked, turn.

Row 3: Sc in each of first 16 [18, 20] sc, leaving rem st unworked, turn.

Row 4: Sc in each sc to last sc, leaving last sc unworked, turn.

Rows 5–10: Rep row 4. *(8 [10, 12] sc at end of row 10)*

HEEL TURNING

Row 11: Sc in each sc across, sc in unworked sc at ends of rows 8 and 6, sl st in side of last st in row 5, turn.

Row 12: Sk sl st, sc in each of next 10 [12, 14] sc, sc in unworked sc at ends of rows 9 and 7, sl st in side of last st in row 6, turn.

Row 13: Sk sl st, sc in each of next 12 [14, 16] sc, sc in unworked sc at end of row 4, sl st in side of last st in row 3, turn.

Row 14: Sk sl st, sc in each of next 13 [15, 17] sc, sc in unworked sc at end of row 5, sl st in side of last st in row 4, turn.

Row 15: Sk sl st, sc in each of next 14 [16, 18] sc, sc in unworked sc at end of row 2, sl st in side of last st in row 1, turn.

Row 16: Sk sl st, sc in each of next 15 [17, 19] sc, sc in unworked sc at end of row 3, sl st in side of last st in row 2, turn.

Row 17: Sk sl st, sc in each of next 16 [18, 20] sc, sc in side of last st in row 1, sc in each of next 18 [22, 22] sts of Cuff, sl st in side of last st in row 1. *(36 [40, 44] sc)*

FOOT

Sc in each sc around until piece measures 5 [6, 7] inches from base of Cuff or 2 inches shorter than length of wearer's foot.

TOE

Fold piece flat, having ends of Heel rows at side folds. Place marker in st at each fold having 17 [19, 21] sts between markers.

*Sc in each sc to 2 sc before next marker, **sc dec** *(see Stitch Guide)* in next 2 sc, sc in marked st, sc dec in next 2 sc, rep from * until 14 [16, 18] sc remain. Fasten off, leaving a 12-inch end for sewing.

FINISHING

Turn Sock inside out. Sew end of Toe opening closed. ■

Pink Taffy

SKILL LEVEL

INTERMEDIATE

FINISHED SIZES

Instructions given fit size small *(women's shoe size 6–7)*; changes for size medium *(women's shoe size 8–10)* and size large *(women's shoe size 12–14)* are in [ ].

MATERIALS

- Lion Brand Microspun light (DK) weight yarn (2½ oz/168 yds/70g per ball):
  2 [2, 3] balls #146 fuchsia
- Size F/5/3.75mm crochet hook or size needed to obtain gauge
- Tapestry needle
- Stitch markers

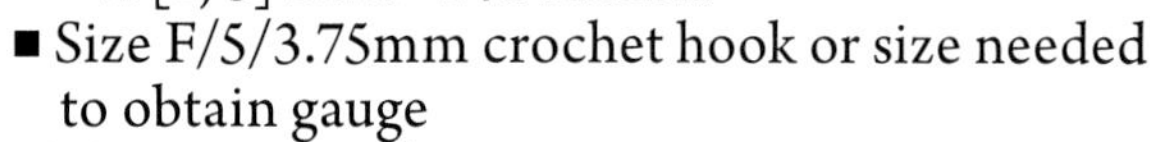

GAUGE

18 sc = 4 inches; 18 sc rows = 4 inches
Take time to check gauge.

PATTERN NOTE

Weave in ends as work progresses.

SPECIAL STITCHES

Beg single crochet foundation stitch (beg sc foundation st): Ch 2, insert hook in 2nd ch from hook, yo, draw lp through, yo, draw through 1 lp on hook *(base ch)*, yo, draw through 2 lps on hook.

Single crochet foundation stitch (sc foundation st): Insert hook in base ch of indicated st, yo, draw lp through, yo, draw through 1 lp on hook *(base ch)*, yo, draw through 2 lps on hook.

INSTRUCTIONS

SOCK

MAKE 2.

CUFF

Note: *Cuff is worked in continuous rnds.*

Beg sc foundation st *(see Special Stitches)*, 41 [45, 49] **sc foundation sts** *(see Special Stitches)*, being careful not to twist sts, join with sc in first st.

Working in continuous rnds, *sk next st, 3 sc in next st, sk next st, sc in next st, rep from * around until piece measures 6 inches from beg.

INSTEP

Work 32 [35, 37] sts in pattern, ch 24 [25, 28], sk next 21 [23, 25] sts *(heel opening)*, continue in pattern around. *(45 [48, 53] sts)*

Work as for Cuff until piece measures 11 [12, 14] inches from beg or 2 inches shorter than length of wearer's foot.

TOE

Lay piece flat with 1 end of heel opening on each side, sc in each st to fold, place marker, sc in each of next 22 [24, 26] sc, place marker, ***sc dec** *(see Stitch Guide)* in next 2 sc, sc in each sc to 2 sc before next marker, sc dec in next 2 sc, sc in marked sc, rep from * until 12 [16, 20] sts remain. Fasten off.

HEEL

Join yarn with sl st at 1 side of heel opening, work 46 [48, 54] sc around opening. **Do not join.** Place marker, sc in each of next 23 [24, 27] sc, place marker, *sc dec in next 2 sc, sc in each sc to 2 sc before next marker, sc dec in next 2 sc, sc in marked sc, rep from * until 12 [16, 20] sc remain. Fasten off, leaving a 12-inch end for sewing.

FINISHING

Turn Sock inside out. Sew Heel and Toe openings closed. ■

Candy Stix

SKILL LEVEL

INTERMEDIATE

FINISHED SIZES

Instructions given fit size small *(women's shoe size 6–7)*; changes for size medium *(women's shoe size 8–10)* and size large *(women's shoe size 12–14)* are in [ ].

MATERIALS

3 LIGHT

- Moda Dea Sassy Stripes light (light worsted) weight yarn (1¾ oz/147 yds/50g per ball):
  2 [2, 3] balls #6946 crush
- Size E/4/3.5mm crochet hook or size needed to obtain gauge
- Tapestry needle
- Stitch markers

GAUGE

17 sc = 4 inches; 18 sc rows = 4 inches
Take time to check gauge.

PATTERN NOTE

Weave in ends as work progresses.

INSTRUCTIONS

SOCK

MAKE 2.

TOE

Note: *Toe is worked in continuous rnds. After placing markers, move them as you come to them.*

Ch 9 [9, 11], sc in 2nd ch from hook, sc in each of next 6 [6, 8] chs, 3 sc in next ch, place marker in 2nd sc of 3 sc just made, working in unused lps on opposite side of beg ch, sc in each of next 6 [6, 8] lps, 2 sc in last lp, place marker, *2 sc in next sc, sc in each sc across to 1 sc before marker, 2 sc in next sc, sc in marked sc, rep from * until there are 36 [40, 44] sc, sc in each sc to next marker.

FOOT

Note: *Foot is worked in continuous rnds.*

FOR SIZE SMALL ONLY

Rnd 1: Sc in each of next 2 sc, **fpdc** *(see Stitch Guide)* around next sc 2 rnds below, sk sc behind fpdc, *sc in each of next 4 sc, fpdc around next sc 2 rnds below, rep from * once, sc in each sc around to first fpdc.

Rnd 2: *Sc in next fpdc, fpdc around next sc 2 rnds below, sc in each of next 3 sts, rep from * twice, sc in each sc around to first fpdc.

Rnd 3: Rep rnd 2.

Rnd 4: *Sc in next fpdc, fpdc around next sc 2 rnds below, sc in each of next 3 sts, rep from * twice, sc in each sc around to last 4 sc before first fpdc.

Rnd 5: *Fpdc around next sc 2 rnds below, sc in each of next 4 sts, rep from * 3 times, sc in each sc around to first fpdc.

Rnd 6: *Sc in next fpdc, fpdc around next sc 2 rnds below, sc in each of next 3 sts, rep from * 3 times, sc in each sc around to first fpdc.

Rnds 7–9: Rep rnd 6.

Rnd 10: *Sc in next fpdc, fpdc around next sc 2 rnds below, sc in each of next 3 sts, rep from * 3 times, sc in each sc around to 4 sc before first fpdc.

Rnd 11: Rep rnd 5.

Rnds 12–16: Rep rnd 6.

Rnd 17: Rep rnd 10.

Rnd 18: Rep rnd 5.

Rnd 19: Rep rnd 10.

FOR SIZE MEDIUM ONLY

Rnd 1: *Sc in each of next 4 sc, **fpdc** *(see Stitch Guide)* around next sc 2 rnds below, sk sc behind fpdc, rep from * twice, sc in each sc around to first fpdc.

Rnd 2: *Sc in next fpdc, fpdc around next sc 2 rnds below, sc in each of next 3 sts, rep from * twice, sc in each sc around to first fpdc.

Rnd 3: Rep rnd 2.

Rnd 4: *Sc in next fpdc, fpdc around next sc 2 rnds below, sc in each of next 3 sts, rep from * twice, sc in each sc around to last 4 sc before first fpdc.

Rnd 5: *Fpdc around next sc 2 rnds below, sc in each of next 4 sts, rep from * 3 times, sc in each sc around to first fpdc.

Rnd 6: *Sc in next fpdc, fpdc around next sc 2 rnds below, sc in each of next 3 sts, rep from * 3 times, sc in each sc around to first fpdc.

Rnds 7–9: Rep rnd 6.

Rnd 10: *Sc in next fpdc, fpdc around next sc 2 rnds below, sc in each of next 3 sts, rep from * 3 times, sc in each sc around to 4 sc before first fpdc.

Rnd 11: Rep rnd 5.

Rnds 12–16: Rep rnd 6.

Rnd 17: Rep rnd 10.

Rnd 18: Rep rnd 5.

Rnds 19–21: Rep rnd 6.

Rnd 22: Rep rnd 10.

FOR SIZE LARGE ONLY

Rnd 1: Sc in each of next 6 sc, **fpdc** *(see Stitch Guide)* around next sc 2 rnds below, sk sc behind fpdc, *sc in each of next 4 sc, fpdc around next sc 2 rnds below, rep from * once, sc in each sc around to first fpdc.

Rnd 2: *Sc in next fpdc, fpdc around next sc 2 rnds below, sc in each of next 3 sts, rep from * twice, sc in each sc around to first fpdc.

Rnd 3: Rep rnd 2.

Rnd 4: *Sc in next fpdc, fpdc around next sc 2 rnds below, sc in each of next 3 sts, rep from * twice, sc in each sc around to last 4 sc before first fpdc.

Rnd 5: *Fpdc around next sc 2 rnds below, sc in each of next 4 sts, rep from * 3 times, sc in each sc around to first fpdc.

Rnd 6: *Sc in next fpdc, fpdc around next sc 2 rnds below, sc in each of next 3 sts, rep from * 3 times, sc in each sc around to first fpdc.

Rnds 7–9: Rep rnd 6.

Rnd 10: *Sc in next fpdc, fpdc around next sc 2 rnds below, sc in each of next 3 sts, rep from * 3 times, sc in each sc around to 4 sc before first fpdc.

Rnd 11: Rep rnd 5.

Rnds 12–16: Rep rnd 6.

Rnd 17: Rep rnd 10.

Rnd 18: Rep rnd 5.

Rnds 19–23: Rep rnd 6.

Rnd 24: Rep rnd 10.

Rnd 25: Rep rnd 5.

Rnd 26: Rep rnd 6.

Rnd 27: Rep rnd 10.

HEEL

Row 1 (RS): Sc in each of next 4 sc, *sc in next fpdc, fpdc around next sc 2 rnds below, sc in each of next 3 sts, rep from * 3 times, sc in each of next 16 [18, 20] sc, leaving rem sts unworked, turn.

Row 2: Sc in each of first 17 [19, 21] sc, turn. *(17 [19, 21] sc)*

Row 3: Sc in each sc to last sc, leaving last sc unworked, turn.

Rows 4–11: Rep row 3. *(8 [10, 12] sc at end of row 11)*

Row 12: Sc in each sc across, working across side, draw up lp in end of row 10, draw up lp in unworked sc at end of row 9, yo, draw through 3 lps on hook, sl st in end of next row, turn. *(9 [11, 13] sc)*

Row 13: Sk sl st, sc in each sc across, draw up lp in end of next row, draw up lp in unworked st at end of next row, yo, draw through 3 lps on hook, sc in end of next row, sl st in unworked sc at end of next row, turn. *(11 [13, 15] sc)*

Row 14: Sk sl st, sc in each sc across, draw up lp in end of next row, draw up lp in next unworked st, yo, draw through 3 lps on hook, sl st in end of next row, turn. *(12 [14, 16] sc)*

Rows 15–18: Rep row 14. *(16 [18, 20] sc at end of row 18)*

Row 19: Sk sl st, sc in each sc across, draw up lp in end of next row, draw up lp in next unworked st, yo, draw through 3 lps on hook, sl st in end of next row. **Do not turn.**

ANKLE

Note: *Ankle is worked in continuous rnds. When making 2nd sock, make sure ankles are same length.*

FOR SIZE SMALL ONLY

Rnd 20: Sc in each sc to next fpdc, *sc in next fpdc, fpdc around next sc 2 rnds below, sc in each of next 3 sts, rep from * twice, sc in next fpdc, fpdc around next sc 2 rnds below, sc in next st, draw up lp in end of row 1 of Heel, draw up lp in next sc, yo, draw through all 3 lps on hook, **sc dec** *(see Stitch Guide)* in next 2 sts, sc in each sc around to last sl st of row 1 of Heel, sk sl st, [sc dec in next 2 sts] 3 times. *(34 sts)*

FOR SIZES MEDIUM & LARGE ONLY

Rnd [23, 28]: Sc in each sc to next fpdc, *sc in next fpdc, fpdc around next sc 2 rnds below, sc in each of next 3 sts, rep from * twice, sc in next fpdc, fpdc around next sc 2 rnds below, sc in next st, draw up lp in end of row 1 of Heel, draw up lp in next sc, yo, draw through all 3 lps on hook, sc in each sc around to last sl st of row 1 of Heel, sk sl st, [**sc dec** *(see Stitch Guide)* in next 2 sts] [2, 1] times. *([39, 44] sts)*

FOR ALL SIZES

Rnd 21 [24, 29]: Sc in each sc to next fpdc, *sc in next fpdc, fpdc around next sc 2 rnds below, sc in each of next 3 sts, rep from * twice, sc in next fpdc, fpdc around next sc 2 rnds below, **sc in each of next 4 sc, fpdc around next sc 2 rnds below, rep from ** around.

Continue working in continuous rnds in established pattern to end of skein or to desired length of cuff.

At end of last rnd, join with sl st in first sc. Fasten off. ■

TOLL-FREE ORDER LINE or to request a free catalog (800) 582-6643
Customer Service (800) 282-6643, **Fax** (800) 882-6643

Visit DRGnetwork.com.

ISBN: 978-1-59012-222-8 All rights reserved. Printed in USA 1 2 3 4 5 6 7 8 9

Stitch Guide

For more complete information, visit **FreePatterns.com**

ABBREVIATIONS

beg	begin/begins/beginning
bpdc	back post double crochet
bpsc	back post single crochet
bptr	back post treble crochet
CC	contrasting color
ch(s)	chain(s)
ch-	refers to chain or space previously made (i.e. ch-1 space)
ch sp(s)	chain space(s)
cl(s)	cluster(s)
cm	centimeter(s)
dc	double crochet (singular/plural)
dc dec	double crochet 2 or more stitches together, as indicated
dec	decrease/decreases/decreasing
dtr	double treble crochet
ext	extended
fpdc	front post double crochet
fpsc	front post single crochet
fptr	front post treble crochet
g	gram(s)
hdc	half double crochet
hdc dec	half double crochet 2 or more stitches together, as indicated
inc	increase/increases/increasing
lp(s)	loop(s)
MC	main color
mm	millimeter(s)
oz	ounce(s)
pc	popcorn(s)
rem	remain/remains/remaining
rep(s)	repeat(s)
rnd(s)	round(s)
RS	right side
sc	single crochet (singular/plural)
sc dec	single crochet 2 or more stitches together, as indicated
sk	skip/skipped/skipping
sl st(s)	slip stitch(es)
sp(s)	space(s)/spaced
st(s)	stitch(es)
tog	together
tr	treble crochet
trtr	triple treble
WS	wrong side
yd(s)	yard(s)
yo	yarn over

Chain—ch: Yo, pull through lp on hook.

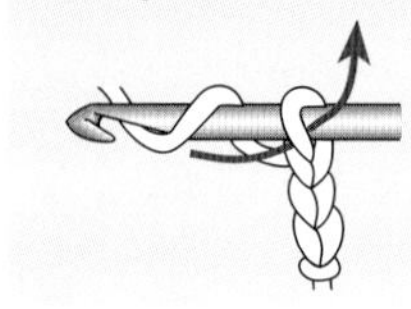

Slip stitch—sl st: Insert hook in st, pull through both lps on hook.

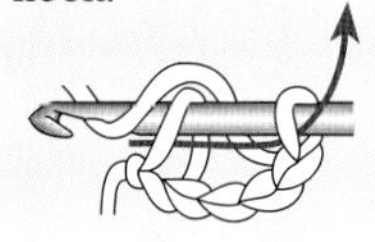

Single crochet—sc: Insert hook in st, yo, pull through st, yo, pull through both lps on hook.

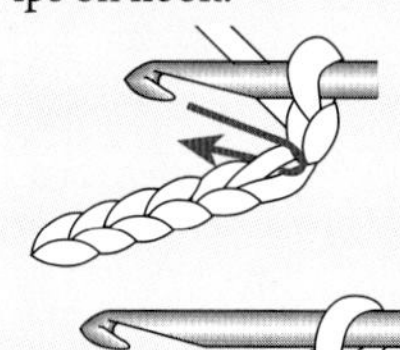

Front post stitch—fp:
Back post stitch—bp: When working post st, insert hook from right to left around post st on previous row.

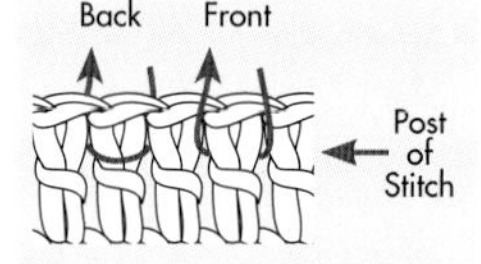

Front loop—front lp
Back loop— back lp

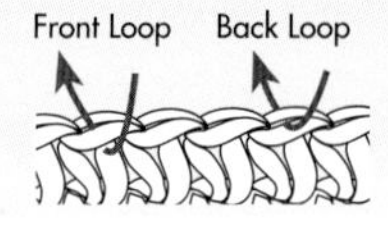

Half double crochet—hdc: Yo, insert hook in st, yo, pull through st, yo, pull through all 3 lps on hook.

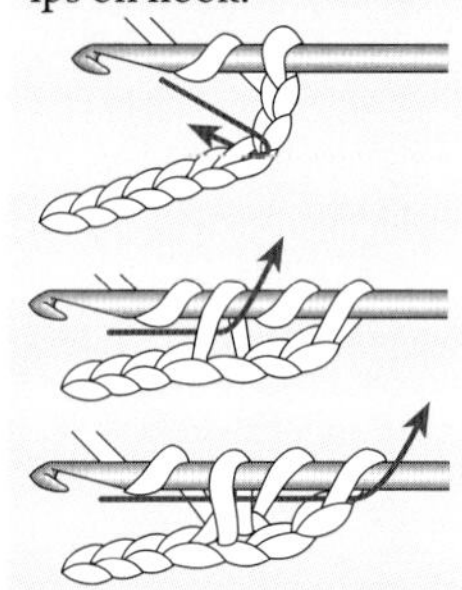

Double crochet—dc: Yo, insert hook in st, yo, pull through st, [yo, pull through 2 lps] twice.

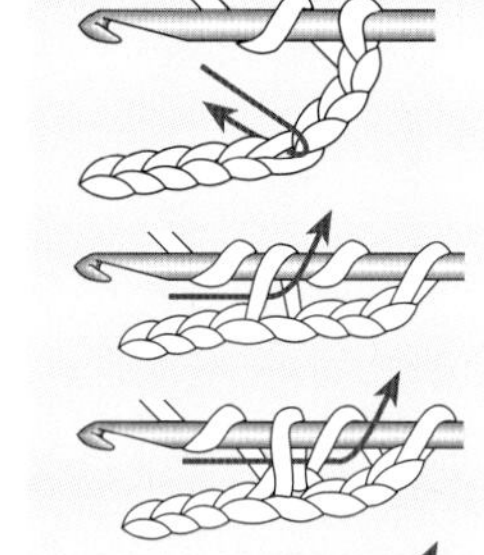

Change colors: Drop first color; with 2nd color, pull through last 2 lps of st.

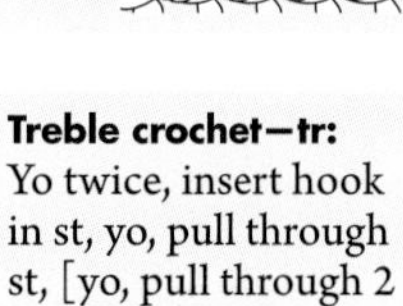

Treble crochet—tr: Yo twice, insert hook in st, yo, pull through st, [yo, pull through 2 lps] 3 times.

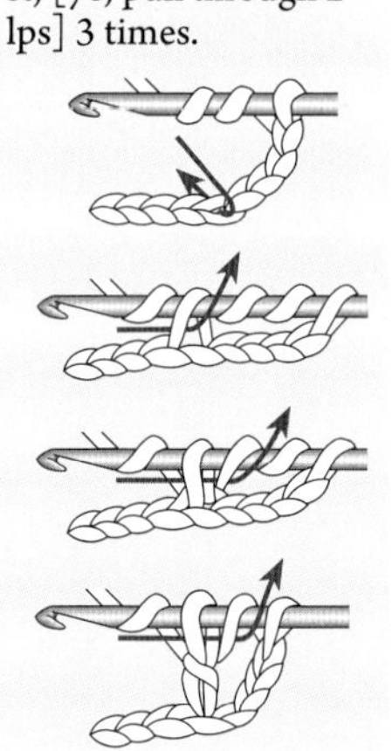

Double treble crochet—dtr: Yo 3 times, insert hook in st, yo, pull through st, [yo, pull through 2 lps] 4 times.

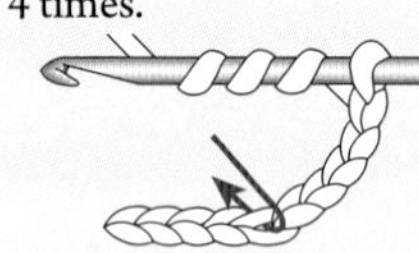

Single crochet decrease (sc dec): (Insert hook, yo, draw lp through) in each of the sts indicated, yo, draw through all lps on hook.

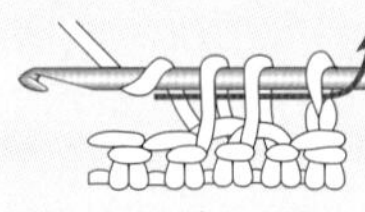

Example of 2-sc dec

Half double crochet decrease (hdc dec): (Yo, insert hook, yo, draw lp through) in each of the sts indicated, yo, draw through all lps on hook.

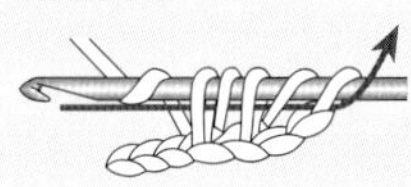

Example of 2-hdc dec

Double crochet decrease (dc dec): (Yo, insert hook, yo, draw loop through, draw through 2 lps on hook) in each of the sts indicated, yo, draw through all lps on hook.

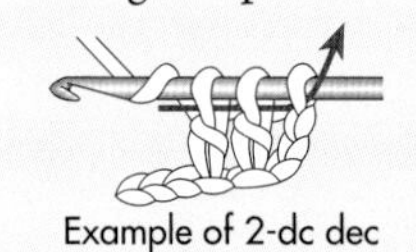

Example of 2-dc dec

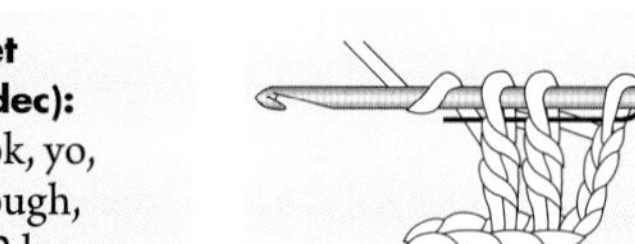
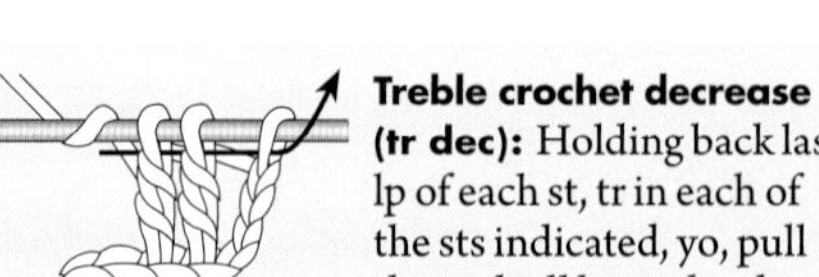

Example of 2-tr dec

Treble crochet decrease (tr dec): Holding back last lp of each st, tr in each of the sts indicated, yo, pull through all lps on hook.

US		**UK**
sl st (slip stitch)	=	sc (single crochet)
sc (single crochet)	=	dc (double crochet)
hdc (half double crochet)	=	htr (half treble crochet)
dc (double crochet)	=	tr (treble crochet)
tr (treble crochet)	=	dtr (double treble crochet)
dtr (double treble crochet)	=	ttr (triple treble crochet)
skip	=	miss